In the Hush

For my family, each one journeying into life,
and especially for Mavis and Millie, in their silence—
the river runs through them,
a finely embroidered thread of hearts and minds.

ACKNOWLEDGMENTS

Thank you to the following journals where these poems first appeared, some
in slightly different versions:

The Barefoot Review, on-line December 2012: "What She Listens For;"
"Journey to Stockton;" "My Sister Sends Field Notes on Our Mother"
The Binnacle, First Prize Poetry Division, Ultra Short Competition, July
2013: "Determined Fish"
Cream City Review, Winter 2010: "Destination: Irony"
Literary Mama, on-line May 2011: "Daughters"
The Mom Egg, on-line 2011, 2013: "In Our Own Particular Fairy Tale;"
"The Far Country of Your Mind"
Orbis, Issue #164, 2013: "The Sentinel"
Sakana, Issue #3, 2004: "Before the Rain"
Sixfold, on-line July 2013: "Alice, Returning;" "The Laws of Motion on
Acacia Street;" "In the Hush of Late Afternoon;" "Just a Little Death"

I sincerely wish to thank the following writers and poets who provided
invaluable commentary on these poems and without whose help, this
chapbook would not have come into being: Mavis Morse-Corman,
Christina Diebold, Shirley A. Glubka, Joseph Morse, and Judith Skillman.

Publisher: Leah Maines
Editor: Christen Kincaid
Cover Art: Susan Woods Morse
Author Photo: Joe Morse

Printed in the USA on acid-free paper.
Order online: www.finishinglinepress.com
              also available on amazon.com

Author inquiries and mail orders:
Finishing Line Press
P. O. Box 1626
Georgetown, Kentucky 40324
U. S. A.

Table of Contents

Section I: Cutting Ties.. 1
The River (An Andy Goldsworthy Moment)...................................... 2
Before the Rain 3
In Our Own Particular Fairy Tale.. 4
The Unwinding.. 5
You Don't Need to Keep Talking at Me, I Already Know You're
    Going.. 6
Tricky Business 7
Lost in Wasco.. 8
Final Wrap... 9
The Laws of Motion on Acacia Street 10

Section II: Meditations... 11
Middle Age.. 12
Alice, Returning.. 13
Sisters' Bedtime Stories.. 14
Suspended... 15
As Sisyphus Rolls that Rock... 16
In the Hush.. 17
The Words She Can't Control 18
Still Life... 19
Daughters 20
Just a Little Death 21
Destination: Irony 22

Section III: Soundings.. 23
Determined Fish.. 24
The Sentinel.. 25
80th Birthday 26
What Is the Sound of One Hand Clapping? 27
The Far Country of Your Mind... 28
What She Listens For 29
My Sister Sends Field Notes 30
The Close of a Season... 31
Journey to Stockton.. 32

Notes 33

"A taste for irony has kept more hearts from breaking
than a sense of humor,
for it takes irony to appreciate the joke which is on oneself."

(Jessamyn West in *To See the Dream*, 1957; goodreads.com)

I stored all the bright words, all these long years,
in the back of a dark cave.
And now, being summoned,
they come scratching and stumbling over each other,
out into the bright light of this white page.

Mavis Hess Chaney
(unpublished poem by the author's aunt)

I. Cutting Ties

The River (An Andrew Goldsworthy Moment)

Rafts of golden leaves
from birch and maple
line each bank.

The tide reaches its finger
into the mouth of the water
and gently draws them out.

What if all passages could be so easy,
swelling lightly on the ebb and flow,
the forward glide of water?

Before the Rain

Children at the beach hop up and down,
excited by water, exotic birds in tropical suits,
happy dancers. The adults, ponderous
as ostriches, bury themselves in sand.
Clouds gather on the far shore.

One boy turns the merry-go-round—
rusted spokes in the great iron wheel grate,
crunching bits of sand into fine white crumbs
faster than time can do the job.

A woman with an inward curve to her chin and a slight lisp
hides her shyness and attends to her husband, much older,
who is nodding. A creamy froth of senility moistens his lips,
while she gags against old age.

How is it that our spirits rage against each other
as if the whole world had tilted on its liquid ear,
while children and clouds meet effortlessly and pass
right through the eye of the needle, surfing the wind?

The young children continue to hop
as the older ones, almost grown
into their cages, feel flightless.
They barter against time,

while clouds, ripe with intention,
fly like round bellies of madonnas,
flaunting the heavens.

In Our Own Particular Fairy Tale

In the kitchen you peel ripe mangoes.
You carve at least a dozen ribbons, scraping
yellow flesh to expose the underlying pulp.

How carefully you strip away the skin. I watch,
knowing that tomorrow you will be gone again.

****

Twice each year we drive to the airport.
You leave either in sweltering humidity or midwinter
under needles of ice. Maine doesn't deal its seasonal blows
in diminutives. Pale as a hung moon, you hug us good-bye.
I turn from your smile to the safety of our car.

Daily phone calls dwindle. *Face the music, fat lady,*
you seem to say. *This kite flies just fine by itself,*
or your favorite, *I've already blown this popsicle stand.*
Your leave-takings become waiting—waiting for you to come,
waiting for you to go. No one holds the trump.
We're a family of great pretenders, carrying on
our night-before-you-leave dinners and Santa cookies
long after they are even a decent lie.

****

Today you keep peeling soft flesh.
I stare at the damn skins which clutter
the kitchen sink and listen to your casual whistle.
I look anywhere but at the hard set of your face.
I just know bruising will occur.

The Unwinding

I'm trying to loosen impenetrable thread,
no, just trying to hem your jeans.
They're tight, sequined, stretchy to fit your curves,
but I keep running into a hitch.
Old thread clogs the bobbin.
I start unwinding layers. Each has its history.
There is hot pink and then a pale green
once like new leaves.
I wonder what dress or soft nightgown
I sewed with it many years ago.
The hardest one is knotted, intricate,
white which has yellowed with time.
Clumps of tangled threads drop to the floor.
The cat pounces in and out.
Even knotted bits of thread amuse him.
Sitting by the door, he waits for your return,
missing you, as I do.

So I'm frustrated this morning
trying to mend your jeans, trying to please.
You've got another date tonight.
The cat and I will watch reruns, but first
I'll have to snip these tiny, complicated strings
down to bare metal.

You Don't Need to Keep Talking at Me,
I Already Know You're Going

You just keep nattering,
nattering in my ear.

I'd like to take my ears,
enclose them in Saran wrap,
and place them in your lunch box
for a late afternoon snack.

Then you could slowly unwrap them,
savor the sounds, the whisper or the snap,
all the while knowing you partake
of an unusual delicacy.

Maybe you would appreciate the curl
that your words must encircle and penetrate.

But right now it's a long, winding journey
to my brain, boxed in ice.

Tricky Business

After you have gone, I gather wood
to the whistle of a marauding wind.
It's as if this sudden change in weather
from the facile days of Indian summer
has stripped me of any pretenses.

Even the cats frisking around my ankles
cling close for all their show of bravado.
Their scampering does not deceive me.

It's no wonder the plants laid out
beneath this undertaker's breeze
could have succumbed so easily.
I should have banked them
in soft earth and downed leaves.

I remember girls in white dresses, dancing
round and round on maple-scented nights.

Capturing memories can be a tricky business.
When we were young, savage mosquitoes
buzzed our summer seasons.

Lost in Wasco

I'm not saying it's bad.
I'm not saying it's good.

But I think of all the surface
conversations we have endured
instead of
the ones we longed to hold,
and somehow never quite got around to.

Was it lack of nerve? Politeness?
Would it have punched us into some corner
forging a 90 degree shift in our relationship?

Did it make us lose something,
something indelible just a hint
below our horizons? Did we lose
any love, or just restless nights
where morning rose up too quickly
to haunt us?

Ah, the things I wanted to tell you,
hoping they would pierce the surface
of your heart,
or at the very least,
your mind.

I never heaved those words into existence.

Instead, I left them slinking, skinny
like an old cat that scrambled hobo-style
from a baggage car into a silent desolation
of weeds and heat in Wasco,
traveling towards a destination
too nameless for either one of us.

Final Wrap

Picture a mediocre horror scene.

> You don't hear the words flying like bats
> from her mouth. Little deaths are like that,
> better viewed with no sound.
>
> Her face now in shadow, as she masters
> the fine art of sidestepping last acts.
> Next take, fear or rage?

Rerun classic 50's cinematography.

> Main character holds babe in arms. Life
> seems to float on mother's lullaby, but soon drifts
> out of focus amid all those deadlines, the daily serials.

Try to fit the perfect family movie into one long-playing reel!

> Endless work takes over, hours of editing.
> But when the film is finished,
> critics descend.

Imagine how your face registers surprise.

The Laws of Motion on Acacia Street

Outside the ER doors at Dameron Hospital
a young woman is dancing strangely.

The circle of traffic is noisy, spinning through the roundabout,
she in the middle of the morning commute.

A whisper of fog is in the air
after last night's rain.

She moves in slow contortions,
perhaps laden with the damping chill.

Her arms struggle with emotion, wave in response
like seaweed about her head.

No sound comes from her lips, or we onlookers may not hear it,
our windows rolled up tight. A few drivers slow to stare.

Others, blind to anything but the daily trajectory,
speed up, racing toward their own destinies.

Two lanes over in the city park
are five shining black crows.

One keeps the focus intense, poised to dip his beak
as night crawlers rise up from the wet ground.

II. Meditations

Middle Age

She carries her heart
like an old wound,
crusted about the edges.

Her smile curls around it,
protective. Her eyes
are hooded, a place where

stories have been tossed.
So this is how she settles into it,
with the comfort of many repetitions.

Alice, Returning

Why did you come back to our valley of illusions?

Did you miss those skies darkened by black peat?
Did you lose your way among rows of dust-cloaked vineyards?
Paths that led to stucco houses with identical doors?
Or did you miss the glass coffin of summer heat?
The family trip that never was?

When we were young, I railed against my tether, belligerent
like a surprised heifer under the ax. I felt the glare of sun,
heard the whir of swamp coolers, dreamed of other fantasy worlds.
While the silent press of summer idled under high tension wires,
those iron ladies-in-waiting pointed to escape,
a lunatic army bent on freedom.

I left, feeling sure then that I could abandon you
and our childhood memories—Dead Dog Corner,
our father smiling into his last beer,
the silence of years between.

So how do you live now, Alice, with your looking glass of tears
and your white rabbits, just so?

Sisters' Bedtime Stories

"Trust me," you said as you proffered a hand.
Being the little sister, she trusted, exposed her palm.
You always said, "I won't do it again,"
and you won her over too easily, each time
jerking her out of bed, knowing
she feared that wolves lived under there.

But tonight you are circumspect, stalling,
in your nightdress. Now her grown-up stories
arrive with punctuality, the weekly blog. Words blur,
black and white shadows of someone else's life.
She is 3,000 miles away. It is late and quiet,
the only time you read anymore.
Hearing of her children's games,
you recall your own, the bedtime ones.
You always won, so predictable.

Before setting a night alarm in the dim hallway,
you pause, her crumpled letter in hand.
You read it once again and smile.
After two movies and a third glass of wine,
you smile easily.

Breaking the stillness of the house,
you put the dogs on guard,
tell yourself it's time to cork the bottle.
You listen for the absent ring of the phone.
This all brings a certain harmony to the evening,
to the safe harbor of anticipated routines.

Then you climb into bed to lie awake,
to travel once more into the slow dawn
of your particular revelations.

Suspended

I don't know if we had been that carefully
considerate of each other for a long time

the night your father died. We handled words
like egg shells. In the window, silhouettes—

our selves traced into the rain's black heartbeat.
We whispered, remembered, quietly conversed,

heads lowered under lamplight at the kitchen table.
Our children were absent—

recognition dawning it was just the two of us,
no padding between.

Each gray hair seemed to have its script memorized,
waiting for entrance, knowing the plaintive melody

"Who knows where the time goes?"
was an epiphany we'd rather not have.

I fooled myself, thinking that I was only reliving
the heartache of my own father's death, 30 years before.

You were stoic, and hell yes, I was stoic.
I'd played this scene before.

But going on a just-to-get-out-of-the-stuffy-house (we said)
ride, when I unexpectedly touched your knee,

I noticed a delicate trembling of your hands,
no longer sure steering our wheel.

As Sisyphus Rolls That Rock

She keeps skirting around the edges
    refusing to fall in.
        The wound is an old crater,
            a depression that won't heal.

        She tries ointments and Band-Aids,
           alternately hiding it,
                then exposing it to bright light.
                She takes a certain pride in it.

                The wound gives her an excuse.

            In the roundness of it,
                the never-ending circle of burned flesh,
           the slight, but always lingering pain, is a scar
      she's found she can't live without.

        The hole is small, a white spot on her conscience.
      She gouges it, so it keeps oozing,
    no matter how many times she then
tries to cover it up.

In the Hush

I sit on our deck, hands clasped behind my head,
contemplating the meaning of "now."
I want to loll like our cat and bask in the heat
with his easy *ennui*,
only mine would be determined detachment,
not the same thing at all.

Instead, like him, I listen to the birds.
We both watch a swallow beat, then rest,
beat, then rest its wings against the paleness of sky.
And I think that is how to do it,
that is how to climb
a long tunnel of hollow air.

Tonight you and I will walk to the neighborhood bar,
telling ourselves we want the exercise,
but I think it is also because the phone rarely rings.
We will each drink one beer to tide us over
for the quiet walk home. We are just
occasional visitors there, unknown.

And for a long time after your snoring has begun
I will gaze through the dormer window
knowing that somewhere in a field
which has a certain false luminescence,
the green that plays tricks when I remember
being young and in the moonlight,
in that field a cow chews its cud, indifferent
to the consuming interests of the heart.

The Words She Can't Control

A single bird lands in the
crevice

just outside her window frame,

trills three notes,
shatters silence.

From deep within this abecedarian's belly, molten pebbles spew.

She tries to rearrange the calendar of her mind, but
random words keep rumbling like chainsaws.

She can't focus on the serendipity of such moments,

her thoughts now a vast ocean, blurs of noise and color.
She's become unmoored,

no longer wholly anchored within the picture she nestles in her mind.

She fancies a spot of red that first converges, then diverges,
flurries, red and black.

A cardinal escapes the belly of the whale,

flits upward through wintry sky,
broadcasting her hunger notes.

Still Life

In the quiet oblivion of middle age
it is with considerate knowledge
that I enter
the attic of my mind.

Tap tap tapping, I rummage,
careful of brown spots that have crept over my hands.

I slowly sift for nuggets, tiny embryos
waiting for the blinding white of life:

Here a sepia photo of my father,
pictures of rosebushes on Calhoun Way,
a white picket fence, plum and nectarine trees
that spread an umbrella of colors across the backyard.

Now a photo taken one summer day I spent gathering
the golden dust of wheat into three Mason jars.

But there is also the ghost of Maggie,
our first Dalmatian, whose silent form follows me
even now. Childhood memories dribble
like dried coffee beans from her lips.

And here is the winter sparrow
shivering upon our window ledge.

Daughters

We met two days after her birthday.
We planned it all for her,
remembering what we had promised.
Quietly sitting around the table, we ate Lebanese eggs,
sipped from dark cups of French coffee.
We discussed details dispassionately.
We felt we were sophisticated,
calculating the number and kinds of pills she might need,
whether or not we should make an extra key to check on her progress
whether she might be lucid when she most needed courage.

We agreed no blame would be placed.
We were very careful with each other.
It had been a long time since we had all been together.
We did not wish it to be a reunion of regret.
But I pushed the eggs around on my plate,
listening to the little clinks of my fork,
allowing bits of yolk to scatter,
then secretly collecting them back again.

Just a Little Death

In the photograph, Maria stares up at me,
wearing a kerchief. She's far away (Romania, she says)
though that's something only the foreign postmark can verify.
She writes that she helped cut off a chicken's head
and ate the soup.
She held its head when the ax fell.
The chicken soup, she says, was made to entertain her;
she's a guest. She asks if sometimes a little soup is indeed
good comfort. She asks would I have had the strength
to wield that ax or to hold that head?
She writes that she is tired of reading Emily Dickinson's nature poems,
with all those dashes,
and asks me which Harvard genius
decided her poetry was amazing
anyway?

These are all questions I cannot answer.

I envision my mother,
her cotton wool head on a block.
I think *what if sometimes a little death*
is better than incoherence
or soundproofed green walls?
I see the fall of the ax, hear how it swoops
down through the cold air
out there somewhere in Romania.
I see the pinwheels of red
that must have arched upwards
toward a thin December sun
like the beginning of a rainbow.

Destination: Irony

Irony is the fact that I composed this poem,
trying to pack (or unpack) several emotions
that I may (or may not) be feeling,
struggling not to lose the lines
while I drove our beat-up, old truck
home from the grocery store, hitting every red light.

Irony presents itself in certain portmanteau words
like suitcase, a place in which you may happily
(or unhappily) be forced for a determinate
(or indeterminate) time to pack your life
and all of your belongings.

I once wrote a poem about a Samsonite suitcase ad.
Picture a single-minded line of black suitcases marching
over the soft breast of a desert sand dune,
perspective, of course, dwindling.
I had thought of how often a continuous stream
of black-suited businessmen might indeed have marched
over centuries of the comforting (or not so comforting)
breasts of real women. The irony of it is
suitcases enable so many beginnings
(or points of departure) that whole personalities
could get swallowed up inside them.

Finally, irony is packing my own bag
(once again) for a return visit to an aging parent
who may (or may not) know me this time.
But I will bring many presents
arranged oh so neatly in that suitcase,
including my many selves, and I will be sure
to repack the delicate articles of both our lives
should they become disturbed in mid flight.

III. Soundings

Determined Fish

She opens her mouth
but no words escape,
her lips pearl gray,
eyes glassed over.
She now spends most of her days in bed,
flopping from side to side
in a woolen river of blankets and dreams
carried by the tide.

I once saw real fish,
jaws thrust forward with determination,
bloated mouths gasping,
swim against such a current,
their scales slaked off,
discarded skins left over in the irrigation ditch
a huge pump was sucking dry.

The Sentinel

Long ago my mother hired an itinerant artist who created paper
cut-outs of all her children. The scissors going snip snip. Our
youthful selves preserved black on white, even the soft curve of
lashes captured upon a sky-white backdrop.

One crow silhouetted against gray morning sky,
black fan of wings and talons,
blowzy cut of tail with a single feather
delicately outlined, a Japanese print.

The sky fashions a halo around the cut of his head.
The crow broadcasts on the silver radio,
"Hurry! Come pluck the little bits of death
scattered along the highway."

Sooner than you think it will be dusk.
He and his companions will swarm
the trees, their chortling reminiscent
of old people's mindless chatter at the end
of a hot haze-and-shimmer day.

And somewhere within this *Neverland*
the old ones scissor along their own tension lines.
Are they also watching, listening
to timeless scolding from black birds,
high-wired between dusk and some new dawn?

80th Birthday

The hard edges of past words tremble
as I talk to my mother on the telephone,

but I have finally come to value
the small treasures unpacked in our attic.

This parade of images might be her salvation:

old wooden stilts, hand-sewn Halloween costumes,
ochre hues of photos captured with a Brownie Instamatic.

A squat Bell dial phone surfaces with staring eyes.
I feel if I could just poke my fingers into the right sockets,

they might reveal a forgotten code, small round wads
of comfort patted into square holes and tucked away.

I might also remember the brown sparrow
flitting moth-like against a winter fog many years ago,

its chirping lost
within the picture window's frame.

What Is the Sound of One Hand Clapping?

Whispering,
the one-armed man will tell you

it's a leaf descending in a winter storm,
the grin of an empty swing when the children have all run away,

ringlets escaping
from the dive of silent fish in stilled waters.

Might it be the noise a glacier makes
inching another micrometer down the slope?

The stillness of the last kiss you will ever receive?
Is it the noise snails make curling into their shells?

Can it only be measured in years,
only be heard when one is alone?

The Far Country of Your Mind

Since you put on your mask of futility
and have retreated,
I no longer call you Mother.

If you speak at all, we do not talk the same language.
I don't want to see your lips flap open
or peer into the dark tunnel of no words.

When your milky eyes search mine,
I turn away
from that vacant lot.

Recently I've begun playing "*Mother May I*"
so I can break all the rules. I sneak

three steps away without your permission,
and then I run and run, determined

no ground swell of memories will trip me up.
But when I reach the safety zone, I stop to wonder

what if both our masks break, and I fall down
that same rabbit hole?

Could you toss me some sign,
even one word, in case I need to find you?

Right now I'm dangling.

What She Listens For

In her room where she rarely hears people's voices
is the sound of dragonflies.
They come buzzing and looping,
disperse, and reform in her dreams.
They're what she listens for,
the music of flight.

What she was capable of
in the green thought of her youth!
Before the years came ravaging,
music was her companion,
and laughter, never
the silence of just waiting.

Now words and faces escape her.
Her skin, her smile, her eyes are finely crinkled.
Her mind has become a paper wallet,
thin, with little content.
So what she listens for is the music of flight,
of dragonflies she knew in another lifetime.

My Sister Sends Field Notes on Our Mother

"When I arrived earlier, the paramedics were in her room, working with her roommate. They took her out on the gurney, but this will make her third replacement."

"She was very sharp witted this morning. As soon as she heard my voice she knew who I was and was able to tell me that she did not know my face, but knew my voice. I took her to the common room for coffee and cookies where another woman was babbling in Italian."

Late June—I am finished staking up the peas and beans.
My mother is far away. She doesn't know my name.
She can't talk to me on the phone.
She thinks my sister is her own mother
                         come back from the dead.

My mother has instinctive energy—plants possess it too.
She still enjoys chocolates, her morning coffee and snack.
Like a tendril seeking sun, she gropes her way to the morning room.
But five minutes later she stares into the black hole of her cup
at the soggy crumbs of doughnut that didn't make it to her mouth,
wondering what *they* put into it, whether they're trying to trick her.

And each autumn the plants dry,
                         then wither in my garden.

The Close of a Season

Golden leaves have fallen,
      leaving trunks barren,
but the old ladies refuse
      to go gentle into that good night.
They slump, whiskered chins murmuring
      into their scant bosoms, scrawny hands
clenched tight to wheelchair arms.

Under the pallid stare of an afternoon moon,
      all are waiting for the reckoning.
A dead raccoon is curled in the roadside ditch,
      his black mask fixed in a permanent grin,
paws indelicately spread-eagled
      to the delight of three crows,
who hop in purposeful excitement.

Journey to Stockton
For Millie

Birds shift uneasily in thickets of dreams. I rise early to examine the ghost
of last night. It's another summer in Stockton. I have come all the way
from Maine to see her, perhaps for the final time, and she knows it.

It's the unsettled quality, this stillness in her house which raises tiny needle
of hair at the very edge of reason. Outside, sirens blast into a hot, dust
wind. Old sycamores weep blind sockets.
Silence spreads its trail right to the front door.

Inside where the walls arch overhead like barren trellises, traces of pas
lives reveal tiny wounds from paintings much arranged, indentations from
lovers' quarrels. Only the brutal threads of skeletons remain,
scrapbooks of many journeys. Each fragile stitch hinged
on the turn of a single word. Whole histories lost.

****

She is on her very best behavior, her watery, hazel eyes worried as she cup
my face between freckled hands and coos softly, asks trivialities. Drivin
unfamiliar roads, we stir up the dust of memories. Her right hand clutche
and quivers, signs her own private language, things she cannot tell me.

Lunch is quiet as she eats her salad one teaspoon at a time. Furtive, hidin
bits of chicken in the napkin on her lap, she tells me she no longer ha
an appetite. I remember a downed butterfly I saw earlier, mapping craz
circles on the sidewalk as I stopped to shelter it from a hungry sparrow.

****

Between journeys I realize there may be one special instant in time whe
I lose my sense of self inside the paperweight of the world, where if onl
for a second I am behind its convex lens. Through those glass walls I se
everything magnified, feel more determined than Alice.

Notes

"The River (An Andy Goldsworthy Moment)"—This poem was inspired after watching an Andy Goldsworthy documentary. He is "a British sculptor, photographer and environmentalist who produces site-specific sculptures and land art situated in natural and urban settings. He lives and works in Scotland." (en.wikipedia.org)

"Alice, Returning"—A swamp cooler is "an evaporative device (also swamp cooler, desert cooler and wet air cooler) that cools air through the evaporation of water." (en.wikipedia.org) Growing up in the heat of the San Joaquin Valley in the 1950's, swamp coolers were our means of air conditioning at the time.

"As Sisyphus Rolls That Rock"—In Greek mythology Sisyphus was a king who was punished for being deceitful. He was forced to roll an immense boulder up a hill only for it to roll down when it neared the top and to repeat this action for eternity, thereby representing the idea of "futility".

"The Words She Can't Control"—The word *abecedarian* was used to begin a writing prompt in a poetry workshop that I attended. According to the Merriam-Webster dictionary, in "its oldest documented English uses in the early 1600s, abecedarian was a noun meaning 'one learning the rudiments of something'; it specifically referred to someone who was learning the alphabet." (https://www.merriam-webster.com/dictionary/abecedarian)

Susan Woods Morse grew up in California and then moved to Maine in the early 1980's. She earned a Masters degree in Literacy Education at the University of Maine, Orono, and subsequently taught English Language Arts at the middle school level in rural Maine.

Susan and her husband raised two daughters in Maine, both of whom moved back to the West Coast after they graduated from college. The effects of distance on relationships, plus dealing with relatives who have succumbed to Alzheimer's disease, have influenced the poems in this collection, which ultimately seek to explore rites of passage. In April 2016, Susan and her husband moved to the Willamette Valley in Oregon to be closer to family members. *In the Hush* is her first chapbook.

She writes poems with a strong sense of *place*, influenced by both her upbringing in the San Joaquin Valley and the contrast of adjusting to New England's climate and to Maine winters. Susan completed an internship with the Maine Writing Project in 2004, attended the Fall Maine Writers and Publishers Alliance poetry conference at the Haystack Mountain School of Crafts in Deer Isle, as well as Stonecoast Writers' Conference through the University of Southern Maine. Her poems have appeared in various journals, including *Cream City Review, The Mom Egg, The Aurorean, Literary Mama, Sakana, Orbis, Sixfold, The Barefoot Review, Lynx Eye,* and *The Acorn.* Her poem "Determined Fish" won the Prize for Best Poetry in *The Binnacle*'s Annual Ultra-Short Competition in 2013.

CPSIA information can be obtained
at www.ICGtesting.com
Printed in the USA
BVHW031133050619
550226BV00001B/194/P

9 781635 349344